You Are the Audience
A Year of Going to Performances
David Macpherson

You Are the Audience
Copyright 2024 David Macpherson
All rights reserved
macphersondavid607@gmail.com
100pagedash.wordpress.com
On facebook David's group is Dave Macpherson is a Writing Stuff.
Instagram DavidScottMacpherson

Who Are You

She asks me, "You a friend of the band?"

"No."

"Are you a musician too?"

"No."

She pauses. Her mouth open. "Wait. You just came to hear the music? That's it?"

"Yes. That's it."

"Wow. You are an audience member."

"We are a rare breed," I say.

You Are the Audience

The following are essays about all the performances I went to From April, 2023 to March 2024

April 14, 2023
The Stone Church, Brattleboro, Vermont
Club d'Elf

In April, I went to Brattleboro Vermont for a writing weekend. I did write, but I saw a lot of events. On the first night, I saw a concert at the Stone Church. The band was Club d'Elf. They are a Boston based trance band. I think that's what they are. What is very cool about them is that the line-up changes from performance to performance. They have a large cadre of performers they can call to do a show. Most of the music is completely improvised.

After a relatively uninteresting opening band, I went back to my hotel, thinking I was too tired to see the band, but I paid to see Club d"elf, and dammit, I was going to go see them. When I got back to the Stone Church venue, they were already performing. The music was cool. Sometimes the improvisations were wonderful, other instances they were head scratching. But it was engaging.

In ninety minutes, they had done three musical pieces. This is just to give you an idea that they were in no rush to get to the next thing. I had a pretty good time being enveloped by the music. Other people were leaving. There were considerably less people there at the end then when they started and I couldn't figure out why people would leave. The music was good. It was challenging, but fun.

They finished their set. They bowed. They left the stage. I was happy with the show. Then they came back for an encore. And at that I said to myself, "Oh, hell no!" I turned and headed to the door. Walking at the back of the venue, I went by the merch table. I was leaving before they were done, but I still liked the band. I bought their double LP set.

I listened to it the next day and I hate to say this, but I liked the way the music was on the record more than I liked it live. What does that mean? Isn't live music the ultimate expression? Did I get a slightly off night of music? I liked the show, but the album is terrific. I feel like I am saying something blasphemous. But there we are. And if I want someone to understand the cool weirdness of Club d'Elf I can play them the album. "They are like that if you see them, but different."

April 15, 2023
Next Stage, Putney Vermont
Rani Arbo and Daisy Mayhem

Explaining your songs pisses me off. I don't want you spending five minutes explaining how this song was created, followed by the four minute song. I just want the song. If the song cannot hold my attention without the introduction, then the song has failed. I want the song to be a thing discovered with no past or future. I just want the song to happen.

The folk band was way too sedate for my tastes. Maybe I would have liked that when I was young and wanted to feel restive, but there is too much punk rock in our lives to even spare the folk concert from some energy and anarchy.

Rani Arbo has a lovely voice and is a great musician, but the songs were too laid back. I would have been happier if the concert was shorter. It seems like songs at the end of the night reminded me too much of songs from the beginning.

I am always happy to see music. It is just up to me to pick something that will fit me better. It's not you. It's me.

April 16, 2023

Hooker-Dunham Theater, Brattleboro Vermont

Ernest

I was unsure what to attend this Sunday at 3. There are two events going on. One was a Clown Funeral for a local arts advocate and the other was this play. Of course the Clown Funeral (not really what it was, but also, it was exactly what it was. More on this in the next entry) or go to a production of the play Ernest.

It is actually, "The Importance of Being Earnest," by Oscar Wilde. The fliers state that it has been updated and adapted for modern times. I was curious why an updated version has to lose most of its title. Why did it need to be shorn of "The Importance of Being?"

I finally decided to go because I remembered this was my mother's favorite play and yet I have always found a way to avoid seeing it. I think I might have watched fifteen minutes of it on PBS with her and then found an excuse to split. But now, in a day where I was just trying to experience as much as I could, I figured this was the time to finally see what my mother loved so much.

I missed the first ten minutes of it because I was being indecisive and then I had to high tail it from the other side of downtown. The woman at the counter seemed annoyed that I arrived late and we had to whisper throughout the ticket purchasing. She said she would get me the change for the ticket. Spoiler, I didn't get it, but it's okay, I am playing it off as a five dollar donation.

There was a lot of cross dressing and visuals of people texting each other. Oscar Wilde's work seems to take it in with no issue. The cast was game. One of them proceeded to climb the walls of the theater.

But it just went down to the fact that despite the modern updating, it was still just the Importance of Being Ernest. It was a classic play with very clever lines. Why did the director and producer think that their modern day window dressing allowed them to change the name and say they adapted it from Wilde? Can't we just enjoy the play and leave it at that?

April 16, 2023
Brattleboro Vermont
A Clown Funeral

I don't know how else to describe this. It was not a Clown Funeral, but a clown adjacent memorial. But that doesn't have the right ring to it.

I was in town for the weekend. I had seen bands and plays and I was also thinking about attending this. There were flyers in store windows saying there will be a memorial for a local resident. He was part of the circus arts scene that Brattleboro has and was part of the old weird Vermont.

They were going to celebrate his life with performance, music and a parade through town. I thought of going to it instead of the Earnest play, both starting at the same time. But if you are reading this in order, you will know that I saw the play. I figured that when it was over, the celebration would be done. I guess I didn't understand how clown memorials work. They go on, baby. They go on.

I picked the play, because I know what that is. I can understand it. You buy a ticket and you sit in a darkened theater and watch people put on clothes they don't usually wear and say things someone else wrote for them to say.

A clown funeral was an unknown variable. And sometimes you want the familiar. You want the shit you know will be what you think they will be. You don't want to be surprised or challenged. You want white bread entertainment.

At five on that Sunday, I left the theater and headed to the hotel when I heard band music and people shouting. I followed it to a parking lot. There was somewhere near seventy five people in a parking lot. A third of them was dressed in clown regalia. There was a woman on stilts. There was a punk rock marching band.

They were playing music and singing. People were taking turns doing bits of performance. One of the organizers was near me and she was going from clown to clown, telling them that they were going to get moving and head down the road toward the bridge.

I went back to my hotel room and wrote for a half hour. I heard something and went to the street and the band was approaching. There was a marching band, filled with people you would net expect to be in a marching bad. These people looked like the cool kids who would never be caught dead strapped to a Sousaphone.

They made it to the bridge that led to the Food Co-op and stopped. There was then a weird skit where a creature shouted nonsense sounds into a megaphone and then it was translated on painted signs that the audience read out loud like it was a church service. This must have been done before. When that was finished, they one by one crossed the bridge.

The procession of band and clowns and people swept up in it was around fifty at this point. It was very slow. I went back to my hotel room and wrote for another half hour. I looked out the window and saw the parade of clowns and clown adjacent folk were going to the field by the art museum. I went with them.

When I got there I heard two beards say, "Can you believe this shit?"

"Course I can believe this shit. This is how Brattleboro used to be. Weird and proud."

The anarchist marching band were now having the seated audience make sounds with one of the horn players getting a higher pitch fro them when she raised her horn up into the sky and then low and rumbling from the audience when she placed the horn close to the grass. I did not participate. I don't like being expected to participate. It seemed like fun, but I had my rules to live by .

Behind me, a blonde young man with an expensive bike was on his phone telling his buddies this was the place to be. "Yeah I know. I know we had plans. But this happening. I don't know what it is. But it is happening and you guys should meet me here. Dude. Just come and see for yourself."

Several women sang in an unknown language. Then several performers covered head to foot and making barking sounds performed a version of Pandora's box. When hope was discovered in the box and everyone, not stoned or drunk, applauded. Actually, the people stoned or drunk applauded with the rest of them.

It was time for me to escape again. I discovered I could only do this for small increments of time. I went across the street to the movie theater and went to see the Dungeons and Dragons movie, primarily to have an excuse to eat candy and popcorn.

After the movie, curiosity impelled me to go back to where the parade ended. I knew it was over because I saw people in smeared greasepaint, in groups of two or three, walk away back to the parking garage.

When I got there, only a few people were sitting in front of a waning fire. They were passing bottle of wine to one another. They were telling stories and laughing conspiratorially. The performance was over. The comedy et fine. Just people tired from a long day and a memory of someone who would have loved to have been there.

May 25, 2023
North Brookfield High School Auditorium

Spring Band Concert

I heard one parent comment, "There is not a lot of kids in the band. When Sarah was in the band there must have been thirty kids. Now there are ten or twelve. This school is going to hell."

My wife and I are going to hear our son play drums wit the band. He does well. I didn't know he could do a drum roll, but there he was, doing it just fine. I was so proud. The band was mostly on key and that was a pleasant change from the winter concert when everyone was off time and out of tune. Sometimes we are not interested in quality but just improvement.

For one song, our kid moved away from the drums and accompanied the group from a keyboard. My wife commenced that he was ready to play for all the 80 synth bands. She said, "Flock of Seagulls," and I held back my laugh.

But the best part of the concert was when it was over. Our son was in the hallway with three of the other guys in the band. They decided to start a band. No one plays guitar, but they will figure it out. They also started to decide the band name, but no consensus was achieved. So no name, no one to play certain instruments but a band was agreed on and so they were a band.

As easy as that.

I will go to all their shows. I will be that parent. I only hope they make it far enough to play out, but that's not important. They are a band. They are going to make music.

I couldn't be prouder.

May 28, 2023.
The Parlour, Providence Rhode Island
The Jim Robitaille Trio

I go in a few minutes before the music is to start. I get a diet coke. Let me just say that I am new enough in not drinking that I feel odd everytime I go to a bar and not get a drink. I know. It's just me.

I heard of the band only because I was looking for a live concert to see. This was close enough and I like jazz combos.

They started and they were all improv all the time. It was guitar, bass and drums. It was good. The exploration was exciting and I was into it.

There are not a lot of tables in the room and soon they are filled up. A woman asks if she can sit with me. I say sure. I mean, I would prefer to be alone with music, but this is a club and what should I do, tell her no?

I looked at my phone while listening to the music. And then she started talking to me. I was not expecting this. She told me that she knows the guitarist. She plays with him at wedding gigs. She is a singer and pianist. She does weddings and some times Jim Robitaille is part of the group.

After a little bit more she asks me if I like this kind of jazz. I do. I say so. "This is not what I like. This is too crazy." I didn't think it was crazy. Just nuts enough. "They are doing nicely with playing off each other."

"I am here because I like Jim. He's a great guy."

"He is a good guitarist and the band is doing well."

She thinks on this and says, "The drummer is too overbearing."

I don't know what she means, but figure she will explain and soon enough, I am right.

"Listen to him. He is so loud. He drowns out the other two. You can hardly hear poor Jim. And when the ending of the songs come, the drummer won't let anyone else end. He always has to be the last sound.

Just wait till they finish. He will fight the other two for the right to be the last thing you hear."

And of course she is right. He is the last sound of the song. But isn't it acceptable for the drum to end it? What do I know? But for the rest of the concert, I am very aware of the drummer. Too aware. It is taking me away from listening to the music.

During the second set she decides to try talking to me some more. "It's hard being an independent. I mean when I started, I had two agents setting up the wedding gigs. But they were taking sixty percent. I figured that's not right and I began doing it myself. What a nightmare. I am making the money but now I know why they got so much of the cut. They deal with the band members and all the other shit. Now I have to deal with the brides. I hate dealing with the brides. They are the worst. I never want to work with brides again. My poor boyfriend might never get a chance to marry me because I can't imagine being one of those monsters."

The band does a Coltrane number and I love it. They get the madness and the melody. The guitarist reminds me of Bill Frissel and that's a hell of a complement.

She gets excited and tells me that she just saw that there are flights to nashville for ninety five bucks from Providence."

"I hear Nashville has some music there," I say.

"I have heard that too. I think I am going to buy the ticket. I'm independently employed. I can do what I want."

"Isn't May and June your busy season for wedding gigs?"

She pauses and then says, "Yeah, but I have time."

The set ends and I thank her for chatting with me and leave the club. It was good to hear improvisational jazz. They were good. But that drummer. All I heard was the drummer being overbearing. Damn her for putting that in my head.

June 11, 2023

The Parking Lot of Peppercorns, Worcester Ma

A Singer named Kyle

I am killing time in Worcester for the next couple hours. I decided to walk around Elm Park. Driving there, I pass Peppercorns and see the microbrewery attached to them set up tables in the parking lot and they had a singer.

After some debate, I turn around, park, and walk over to the music.

I hear a high tenor voice singing "Mrs. Robinson." It's a fun song. But it is a weird one to hear crossing Park Avenue. Fifty year old songs about adultery keeps the people happy and snapping their fingers.

Three are people at almost every picnic table. They are drinking beer and talking to one another. They set up cornhole and several are playing. There are children running around each other in ever widening circles.

Am I the only one present to listen to a singer I have never heard of and will not get his name?

The next song is "Shut Up and Dance.: Then it is "Wagon Wheel.: He has chosen soft rock, easy listening is his lane. It's not a bad lane. But you certainly are not going to get to new places any time soon.

He is a young man with a baseball cap turned backwards.

The songs are harmless. The singing is lilting and kind. There is no anger or sex in any thing he sings, including Mrs. Robinson, a song about an affair. That is toothless too.

But we are here on a warm Sunday and we are drinking beer and we are happy to have a real person sing us songs. Troubadour. Balladeer. Guy in the Microbrewery Parking lot. We don't want hard music. We want waterdowned fun and he has given it to us.

We should be more grateful than we are. We should applaud more. We should let him know that this is exactly what the humid air needed. "Shut up and dance with me."

June 17, 2023
Maureen's Jazz Cellar, Nyack New York
The Gary Smulyan Quintet

I went because I was in town and I never went to a basement jazz club before. I feel like I am not a real jazz fan if I have not gone into a basement to watch a jazz combo. Check one more off the list. Now I need to find an old loft where jazz musicians jam until dawn and my card will be filled.

The owner greeted me at the door and he was very intense. He made sure I turned off my phone ringer. It's a good policy, but he was very vigilant.

The place was packed. That is not saying much for a basement. There were about fifty people there. That's still good for jazz.

The owner did not stop his battle against audience noise. He went around the room shushing audience members who were engaging in conversation with their table mates. These were whispers, but I guess the owner believed that the musicians needed to perform under the condition of absolute silence.

He went up to the offender and shushed them.

It took me out of the excellent music because I was worried what the evil jazz librarian would do next.

June 17, 2023
Prohibition River Live, Nyack New York
Social Station

You have left the jazz club before the late night jazz piano bar. You have your limits. You begin to walk to the car, but the evening is cool and pleasant and it is not even ten so you decide to walk around Nyack for a bit.

Turning onto Main Street you hear live music blaring. You aim yourself toward it. The music is synth heavy and dirge like. The singer has a deep baritone with little range. It is like all those post punk bands that you sort of liked when you were a kid. The Birthday Party. New Order. You know, happy bands.

You walk a little more and hear more live music. It is a cover band that is loud instead of good. You turn around and pay the ten bucks to hear the band with the gravel voice singer.

You go up to a second floor and it is sparsely attended. The band, Social Station, are just two people. One singing and playing guitar, the other hitting the bass. The synths and the drums are all pre-recorded.

You don't like pre-recorded music when you go out to hear music. It probably makes you an old fart, but you want live music to be completely live. That is an old paradigm, but you are old and you can't help it.

The bass player is energetic. He is moving around, letting the bass dance. The singer and guitarist has that low baritone that is less like words and more like reading braille as you are prematurely buried six feet under the ground. That is not a complaint. The music is what it is. It is good for the lane they are dancing in.

There is a young woman standing in the middle of the dance floor silently recording the set. She is the girlfriend of one of them.

Later, you will find out that the two bandmates are father and son. You will see the girl selling merch for them at a side table. You hear they are from Washington DC. You wonder if they are happy that they drove so far for such a small turnout.

But people did turn out. You did. You heard the siren song of retro eighties music and you came. One can only hope that others are susceptible to such a lure.

July 1, 2023
Stone Church, Brattleboro Vermont
Beau Sasser's Escape Plan

Did I take the wrong path? Is the trail of sound I walk on the right one, or am I going in circles.

I am in Brattleboro for the weekend, with a plan to see both bands playing at the Stone Church. I know nothing about either. Friday is a jamp band named EDD. They seem to have a prog rock groove with song cycles and spacey things. The other is a collective called Escape Plan on Saturday. They boast a funky vibe.

I don't have to worry about picking the right band if I go to both. It is best to be voracious and not discerning.

But on Friday, after writing and do a few things in the heat, I am too tired for a nine o'clock start time for EDD. I go to bed and sleep hard.

So now, everything rests on Escape Plan.

And they are okay. Actually, some of their extended jams on classic funk and soul are terrific.

I think the issue is me. I want my bands to do original music. I know that is reductive and inhibits who I see. This band is good, but kind of thrown together. The singer is only with them for this small New England tour and the guitarist also seemed to be new too. They were probably a little rougher than usual.

They played a lot of Stevie Wonder, which is not a bad thing at all. But they can never be Srevie Wonder. You can only aspire to the heights of Stevie Wonder. You might say, "It's good for a cover." I must say, their version of Dolly Parton's Nine to Five was pretty fun.

They had chops. It was great for a band to be piano centered. The keyboardist laid down the base with one hand while creating great runs and trills with the other. But in its heart, they are a bar band playing the cool hits.

There is nothing wrong with a bar band. Bar bands are like the blood that runs through all the organs of a bar. They are the transportation from one moment to the next. Don't ever talk bad about a bar band.

But all I was thinking was the band I didn't go see. A band I knew nothing about. "EDD would have their originals front and center." "EDD would have jammed tighter." "EDD would have given me something I have never heard before." That probably is not true, but always the desire. Always the goal. You want something like you have never heard. You want the brilliance you never knew existed.

This is all fallacy. I go to bands in a willy nilly fashion. I pick em and I don't think about em. That has worked well enough so far. This time? I allowed myself a lady and the tiger scenario. Neither of the bands would have been the perfect maiden. Neither of the bands would have torn me to shreds with their razor sharp teeth.

It is still the rush of seeing bands in person. It is still better than the silence of all this indecision.

July 16, 2023
The Parlour, Providence Rhode Island
The Clay Street Quartet

I was texting Foster when I was there listening to the band. I was by myself. I had a table all to my lonesome. There were 10 people there during this day of torrential rain. I could text if I wanted to and no one would stop me.

I told him that the band I was watching had a vibraphone and I thought was pretty cool. He got back to me saying whenever he thinks about vibraphone he thinks of an old soundie film, and he sent me the link.

While I listened to The Clay Street Quartet I played the video without audio. It was a xylophone band from the 1940s. Most of the xylophone players were young women in sequined ball gowns.

While watching their precision playing I had the soundtrack of what we being played right in front of me and I suddenly really enjoyed the band I was seeing.

Before that, I was not sure. I was uncertain.

It was not what I wanted to see that day. In Worcester, there was going to be a punk rock flea market in the parking of Ralph's Chadwick Diner, which is a great music venue in town. Local makers would get a chance to show off their wares and at five o'clock there would punk bands playing. This sounded cool to me. I would get to thrifting with a punk soundtrack. Who doesn't want that to happen?

The weather.

The weather did not want the show to go on.

I could have stayed at home and complained about the rain and that would have bee n a fine show as well. Instead I headed down to Rhode Island and the Parlour. THey seem to always have Sunday afternoon jazz.

There is no way to put it, this band was the backup. THe cute but not very pretty blind date that you get so that you are not a fifth wheel.

Sometimes you just want to listen to music. I might have been happier with the sloppy punk bands I am sure I would have seen, but this was still music.

The problem is that the vibraphone is cool, but laid back by its very nature. You are not going to rock out with a vibraphone. It is background music pushed out to the spotlight.

I was damp and I guess I was not in the right mood for the music. So I texted friends and watched videos while the music in front of me was background.

The music was good. The musicianship was decent. They were new as a combo and you could tell, but it was still heading somewhere. They were just missing the spark I was hoping for. Maybe I was the person who was supposed to bring that spark for ignition. Maybe it is up to me to see them as exciting and then they will be.

Maybe we in the audience are the ones with the power. The quiet fifth member that makes the band what it is.

July 21,. "N 2023
Mechanic's Hall, Worcester Ma
The John Pizarelli Trio

Five minutes before the show was to being, George asked me if there was going to be a lot of people talking during the music.

I wasn't sure what that meant. "Are people going to be talking during the music?"

"Yeah, are the people going to keep on talking while the music is playing?"

"I don't think so," I said, and then thought better and added, "No, they will not be talking. People know to listen to music."

"Just that, this is jazz and isn't jazz the stuff you play in the background?"

And I smiled. I knew what he was saying. "Yeah, I know what you mean, and the last few bands I have seen were definitely background music and not the music to concentrate on, but no, this is good jazz and good jazz you don't talk."

For the rest of the concert, I am hyper aware of people talking around us. Do they know that this is background music and not focus on it music? I really am impressed with this trio and what they do to standards and the piano player is out of his mind in the best way. They can't be background music. This is transporting you somewhere music. Or at least, it is trying to be that way.

But the combo didn't have drums. George has started playing drums and was annoyed when he didn't see a drum kit set up for the show. "How can it be good without drums?" He was joking of course. Well. I think he was joking. I hope he was joking.

But it was not background. The time flew by and I left happy. How can that be the radio in the other room?

August 8, 2023
Town Hall, Jamaica, Vermont
The Amphion Baroque Ensemble

I got there right at seven. I was the last to arrive. The small town hall was packed and there were no seats remaining. I was SRO. I was standing in the back, like I was lucky to see the Stones in a small club and snuck in at the very end.

The concert was on a Tuesday and there is something wonderfully decadent about seeing music on a work day. Like we are doing something naughty. Wonderfully naughty. And necessary.

A few thoughts.

1-I wish musicians of ancient music do not feel they need to explain the instruments or the time it was written. Just lay on the music. I don't want to learn. I want to hear. I want feel. That's a good enough education for me. With that said, I was amazed to hear that the violin was invented around the 18th century. It's hard to think of the violin as a cutting edge piece of musical technology.

2- One of the four musicians played a bassoon. I played the bassoon, back in high school. I did not have any of the skill or acumen required. I also did not practice often. It was hard getting out of the "dying whale" sound I was good at manifesting. To watch this musician, I am filled with jealousy and regret. So this is how the bassoon is supposed to sound? I get it. I will never be able to replicate it, but I get it.

3-The show was a tour of the 100 years of baroque. They started with obscure composers and ended with Bach, Telleman and Vivaldi. The Vivaldi was stunning/ I texted my friends during that concerto typing "Vivaldi for the Win!" No one gets back to me wondering what is wrong with my head. I guess that's just typical, expected behavior from me.

4- This was part of a Baroque music fest. They invited us all to a woman's house for the next evening. There was to be a garden party with music. They told us we all should come. No. I couldn't. It is hard enough being the only one that the crowd is unfamiliar with. Everyone knew everyone. And there was me. How awkward would I be in some stranger's house listening to old music. Being at the town hall was tough enough, and then to be in someone's house, using their bathroom. Just a guy wanting to listen to good music, not a person who wants to find a community.

August 8th, 2023

The Hotel Room at the Putney Inn, Putney Vermont.

Watching the Movie Searching for Sugarman

After finally finding my way back to the hotel from Jamaica Vermont, I got ready for bed and watched a movie on my computer. No one knew I was the audience. But I was. The most important audience.

I had heard of the movie, but did not feel motivated to watch it, until earlier that day. I had walked over to the record store in Putney. IT is a lovely place and I always find records to buy there. I picked up two Bill Frisell albums there that day, but that's not important right now.

The owner and I got into a discussion about movies about music. The arts center in town did a monthly rock movie and he was involved. He said he didn't do much, but he did recommend a movie. Searching for Sugarman. He said they played it and it went over well. He told me a little about it. It was about Rodiquez who's two early 70s albums were a bust when they were released.

But his albums became a huge success in South Africa. The South Africans thought he was dead and they never tried to find him. He was not dead and the movie deals with that as well.

It was a lovely movie. I really thought it was great. I was happy that the record store owner told me about it. I went to sleep thinking of the music I had just heard.

The next day, I saw an article online that said that Rodriguez died the day before.

I watched the movie the day he died.

What is the significance of that? What power did the movie possess? What power did I possess? If I had put off watching the movie for a week, would Rodiguez had lasted longer?

I was the audience. The whole audience. The one watching. The one listening.

August 9th, 2023
Stone Church, Brattleboro Vermont
The Garcia Project

Twenty-eight years to the day, Ray and i were going to a brew house that we were into. I can't remember why. They must have had good looking waitresses.

When we were waiting for a table, I noticed a sign written on the chalkboard. It said, "Grateful Dead Tickets for Sale! Cheap!" Ray read this and shook his head. "That's pretty funny."

I looked at the chalkboard sign and admitted, "I don't get it."

Ray seemed fed up with me. "Jerry Grarcia died today. So Grateful Dead tickets are worthless."

"Was it on the news?" I asked like the idiot I felt.

I thought of that moment today when I went to the Stone Church to see the Garcia Project. I don't like the Grateful Dead. They are thin and unfocused. I don't understand the people that followed them like trust-fund gypsies. But I was in the area for a writing trip and one of the things that has jazzed me of late is this personal mandate to go see as much music as possible. To see it live. Not participate, but to sit in the dark and dig it!

I came to Brattleboro in the middle of the week. I didn't have a lot of choices. The one big one was this band on Wednesday evening. Why a band on a night that is a school night? Because this is the 28th anniversary of Jerry Garcia dying and we must keep the memory alive? Do we?

This band had some interest in me because it was not a cover band of the Grateful Dead but of the Jerry Garcia Band. This was Garcia's side project that was more a blues band than whatever the hell the Grateful Dead is. So they had that in their favor. They also were recreationists.

Each of their concerts was a recreation of a previous Jerry Garcia Band Concert between 1976 and 1995. The set list and all the bells and whistles were recreations.

Why did I find this interesting? Because I am always curious to see what is the most important aspect of creating: is it the creation of the work or the interpretation of it? I know. I really do ponder all of this weird esoteric shit.

There had to be well over a hundred people there and that is good. I always want a band to get an audience. I always want the venue to do well enough that they will continue so that I can go and see more bands, more random music.

I was in a solid blue t-shirt and a pair of jeans. I was too square for the audience. They were in flowing dresses and tie-dyed shirts. I couldn't be a guy at this concert because I didn't have a beard. Every guy had a beard? Is that a Vermont thing or a Grateful Dead Adjacent Cover Band thing?

The band played and they were good. This is a traveling cover band and they definitely know how to get music out of their instruments. But what music did they produce?

Let me get to the stunning conclusion: I didn't make it through the concert. I bailed at the intermission. And it was a good thing that they stopped for that break because I was planning on leaving at the end of the next song.

So did I hate it? No. Not at all. One of the guys going out during the break to catch some air said to a friend, "Man oh man. The band is really smoking tonight. They are tight. They are smoking. You know." I didn't know. That was why I left. Why did I leave?

I just didn't want to hear anymore.

Let's be fair, this was me being open to anything, even to bands and performers I already don't have an affinity for. Jerry Garcia. People love him. But the jazz inspired blues rock jams that he did in the Jerry Garcia Band are just not my favorite.

And then the main issue is the lack of a beating heart.

The musicians were excellent and made some good music, but they were making another person's music. That's fine. Musicians don't have to write their own music to be awesome.

But this is a special case. They are recreating the set lists of a concert performed decades before. I am pretty sure they also recreated the versions of the song down to each guitar solo. Everything this excellent group of musicians are doing is mirroring what others have done. They are a facsimile. They are a hi res scan. The scan gets all the miniature and all the little details of the original, but it does not have the beating heart of the original.

When I was a kid, there was a commercial for Memorex cassette tape. They recorded the great Ella Fitzgerald hitting one of those killer high notes she had and the note was so powerful that a glass broke. They then showed playing a Memorex cassette recording of her singing that not and the recording broke the glass. The final line of the commercial was one of those ancient questions that will never be fully revealed, "Is it live or is it Memorex."

Of course the commercial was a lot of bullshit, but it brings out the debate of the importance of the original and the copy. If the reproduction is good enough, will it be a satisfactory replacement for the original? Can we be happy in a world where everything is copied and redone?

Are we happy with the replica?

In some cases, yes. I will take a nice poster of Hopper's Nighthawks on my wall because I certainly get the original from its art museum internment. And you can't see Jerry Garcia in concert anymore (though the tickets are cheap now), so the option is a group of musicians who will recreate it for you. It will be just like seeing Jerry Garcia.

But it's not.

The musicians are great, but they are not Jerry Garnia, nor would they ever truly wish to be. They just whisk up a souffle of the familiar.

There were a few numbers where i was moving to it and was excited to hear what they are doing, but my head wouldn't let it go. I kept wondering if each of their solos were not per note. They said it was a recreation and so I was trying to figure out how much of it was the art of the music forger.

I guess my issue was that they did not try to be real. Their ultimate goal was to be Memorex. A really good Memorex, but a Memorex in the end. A thing of memory. A thing of nostalgia. A beautiful moment of celebration and tribute. With only the slightest hint of authenticity. Of the chaos of the real.

August 10. 2023
Retreat Farm, Brattleboro, Vermont
Thursday Food Truck Round Up
The Gaslight Tinkers

Retreat Farm is a large space where farming takes place, but so does many community activities. In the summer, Thursdays is a concert with seven or eight food trucks. People come and enjoy the moment. The food was a wide variety of cuisines.

The band is fun as all hell. It is a fusion of Carribean, African, Funk and even a little bit of old school rap. It is goofy and contagious.

They are the perfect band for this kind of get together. They are a little of everything, so they won't alienate anyone. They are the band for every summer on the commons event. On looking them up, that's their thing. You want to see them? Hang out Town Gazebos in the summer and they might show up.

They are talented, they sing Harry Belafonte songs, they will not offend anyone. Are there classes for bands to play town parties to learn how to be. You must be fusion. You must wear loud clothes. You have to embrace the violin and the electric bass. You are all things to all people and you need to swing, baby.

I say these things to myself while I stand in judgment in front of them on stage, but I have no complaints. This is the third musical event in three days and it is my favorite. They are out here to have fun. Who doesn't want music to be fun?

Near the start of their first set, the ran, which had been threatening, came down. It poured for a few minutes and then got into the groove and came down at an even consistent pace. Some of those presents had large umbrellas.

I did not.

I took refuge in the building that was selling gelato, which had a large covered porch. Me and about twenty others were huddled away from the rain.

But we were not the only ones at the concert. We were just the only ones too afraid to get wet. A few dozen people were out in the raid, listening to the music, accepting the idea that rain happens.

One guy, about my age, was barefoot and dancing. He was leaping. He was spinning. He was slowly galloping yonder and fro. He was having so much fun. His eyes were closed and his smile was illuminating.

He was celebrating the weather and the music and the way the wet grass played on his feet. He was free. He was the music.

And I found myself jealous. WOndering why I sequestered myself to the dry porch. There was so much field to dance in. So many raindrops to be dance partners with. Why was I not dancing?

I remember a storyteller once saying, "If you don't dance, you will rust." I felt my joints creak as I waited for the rain to pass by. Like rain tends to do.

August 20, 2023
The Parlour, Providence Rhode Island
The Ryan Kowal Group

1- I don't know if that is the name of the band I saw.

2- They did not introduce themselves. The album for sale just has the name of Ryan Kowal on it.

3- He is the vibraphonist and the composer of the works they played. But there are 10 people in the band. How can that just be called Ryan Kowal? Does that negate the presence of the other nine on stage?

4- They were not on the website. There was no way to know they were playing. Unless you are related to someone in the band. If everyone one in the band brought three people, the place would be packed.

5. You have to take the notion that there will be live music on faith. You have to believe that someone will show up and make something sonic happen. Before I entered the bar, I stopped and listened and didn't hear anything. Could there be a band? Was I mistaken? But I opened the door and there were a football team of musicians on stage waiting for the bus or Godot or for soundcheck to be completed.

6. I was twenty minutes late getting there. The soundcheck didn't finish for another ten minutes, what with the abundance of instruments. Should I be upset that I was only given 90 minutes of music and not the 120 minutes? Absolutely not. Sometimes it is better that they play less. We don't embrace brevity as much as we should.

7. There was a lot of everything on the stage. A vibraphone. An electric vibraphone. A drum kit. A percussion station with a variety of drums and sound making ephemera, a tenor saxophone. An alto saxophone. A baritone saxophone. A French horn. A keyboard. A bass.. Ten. (I just went back and counted all the instruments listed. It's a line-up alright.) And for all of that, there was a musician. 10 players.

8. They started and they were good. I liked it. There were moments when I was enchanted. That's the thing. I want to be enchanted everytime I see a band. I want to be transported somewhere, as long as it is not outside and to my car and then home in disgust.

9. The band leader was the vibraphonist. He said that most of the work was from a suite he wrote about getting and then leaving a cult. Now that's a theme for a jazz suite. I didn't hear the plot in the music I was presented with, but I trust that it was all there..

10. There is a tradition of everyone getting a solo. Some of the solos were amazing. The tenor saxophonist was particularly amazing. I waited for his solos. The alto saxophonist had a scowl the whole time. Maybe that is just his resting face, but it was off putting. It felt like he was not impressed with his fellow musicians. He had resting judgmental face.

11. About an hour in, the leader realized the French horn player had not had a solo. He said, "We can't forget you. Next piece. You solo." I couldn't see her, but I immediately felt one of those moments in grade school where the teacher asks the class a question you have no idea on and so you will yourself to be small and unseen. Maybe the French horn player didn't want to solo. She didn't raise her hand. Just let her be. Let her contribute to the aural feeling of the music. Her solo was ok. I mean, doing a solo ain't easy. It's a different skill that many musicians have not tried. Her solos were just flights up and down the scales. They were not up to what the others were doing. I rooted for her. I got pink in the face. I was feeling performance anxiety just sitting in the audience.

12. When the show was over, I was shocked to acknowledge that this was a great deal of fun. The musicians were not all of the same caliber, but all of them on stage working on a particular vision was great.

13. The leaders of the band said that he had the suite for sale. When I went up to the lonely merch table, I saw the Passages album and pieces of paper. They were a download code. I am an old fogey. I don't download code. I get albums or CDs. I am that old shit who should know better about music and technology. The leader, Ryan, came over and told me

the story. I could get a download code for the album for ten bucks and he would throw in a candle he made. (He makes candles) Or I could get the album, which is a 45 rpm album with only two of the five movements on it, with the download code and a candle for 25 bucks. I just couldn't do it. I wanted the album, but not if it only had a portion of the suite. It didn't make sense and I left without buying anything. Not even a candle.

14. The next day, I found the whole suite (album) on Youtube and I listened to it. I preferred the live version I saw over the album, but that is not uncommon.. I felt bad about listening to it on YouTube. No artist was going to make money from me listening to it there. With all that said, I didn't stop listening to it.

September 3, 2023
The Parlour, Providence Rhode Island
The Monthly Jazz Jam

If you can learn something about yourself when you go to see live music, then it is a successful moment and should be cherished.

I learned something.

I don't like Jazz Jams.

I have been to a few of them, and this evening solidified it all for me.

I don't like them.

What is a Jazz Jam?

This version seems to be a standard version of the phenomena.

There is a basic band who plays throughout. People sign up and they can sit in for two songs. Sometimes they will use the drums or the keyboards (giving the band's player a break), but most of them brought their own horns.

What's wrong with that? The band was good and they kept things moving. So what is there not to like?

A few things.

I have never liked the pause between songs where the band chats and takes a breather and maybe retunes the guitar. I just want a band I see to blaze from one song to the next.

In Jazz Jams, it is worse. The people called up have to make sure the horn is all put together. They need to make sure everything is tuned. Then they need to talk to the band leader to set what song they are going to do. Then the band leader has to make sure the other musicians are ready. Minutes go by as I wait for something to happen. I know I should be patient. But I am not.

Another thing.

There were a few people who played their two songs with the band and then split. Left as soon as they were done. Maybe they had a place to be. Or maybe they think they are king shit saxophonists and listening to other musicians is anathema. I hate that selfishness in performance. It makes me sit there, stewing in displeasure. Yeah. A sour mood is the best way to hear jazz

But wait, there's more.

Not everyone is up to the skills as the others they are playing with. This idea of everyone gets to play is great, but it might not create the best music. Gelling with a combo is not the easiest thing and jams can be more miss than hit.

Some of what I heard was really good. But they had a group playing a jazz version of Day Tripper and, to be kind, it was a mess. Nothing worse than a sloppy Beatles cover.

Oh, I thought of another issue.

The doorman asked if I was planning to perform when I came in. I said I was just going to listen. (one of those audience people we have heard about) and I was asked for the ten dollar cover. That's cool. No problem. But then I heard that people planning on performing in the jam only had to pay five bucks. It pays to perform. The audience? We get to listen and that costs more. I know I am being unbearably bitchy, but its shit like that that stops people from coming to just listen to these events. It does not pay to just listen.

Yeah, I know. Chill out Dave!

But I think if I had to boil it all down, why I don't like Jazz Jams is that I am not sure what a Jazz Jam is. They spoke of it as a community and that you should talk to other players who performed that night.and get to be part of the group.

So is Jazz Jam a place where diverse players can feel a sense of belonging, or is it a show?

Who is the Jazz Jam for? Is it for the musicians to learn and hang with other musicians or is it for the others to listen?

I know. I know.

It can be both.

It should be both.

But this was not presented as a show, but a place where everyone gets to play.

It is the Sunday Jazz version of the participation ribbon.

The standard band was good and they mentioned that several of them are a part of a Beatles tribute band called Funky Submarine where they do funk versions of the Beatles. That sounds great and I will go see that.

But that sounds like a band that is performing for those in the seats and not for themselves.

If you can learn something about yourself when you go to see live music, then it is a successful moment and should be cherished.

Finding the shit you don't like is almost as important as finding the shit that you do.

September 25, 2023
The House of Blues, Boston
The Breeders w/ The Screaming Females

Dear Kim Deal,

I went to the concert for your band the Breeders last night and i had a wonderful time. You sounded great. I particularly loved when you played several songs from your first album, Pod. That is one of my favorite albums of all time. To hear Fortunately Gone in person almost brought me to tears. I adore that song but over the years I have not played it and had forgotten it. So when you started it, it was a wonderful surprise. You were playing a beautiful song I had misplaced in my heart.

And when you started Cannonball, I realized that I had never seen the Breeders live. I always thought I had back in the 90s, but when you started the song, it dawned on me that this was the first time hearing it live. It was weird to admit that though I told people I saw the Breeders, I never did until now. I saw your first band, the Pixies back in 1989. I saw your band, the Amps, that you put together when the Breeders were on hiatus. But never the Breeders proper. It is a long time from 1989 until now to finally see a band that meant so much to me for so long. You did not disappoint.

But you were not my favorite band that evening. Your opening act, The Screaming Females, was the best thing I have seen all year. They showed great musical skills and passion to spare. They killed that stage. I was smitten by the feedback. I had seen a video of them a while back, so I wasn't completely surprised. But I saw a video of the Pixies before I saw you open for the Cure back in 1989. A video does not make you appreciate the audacity of upstaging the main band. You did it in 1989. I was blown away by the Pixies. It is the same feeling when I hear t he

Screaming Females. It was me thinking, "Where have they been in my life? How did I get through the days without this band?"

I am sure you will fogive me for loving another. You really were swell. But you and I (and a lot of other people) have been doing our musician and audience dance for nearly 35 years. Can't we just admit that we are fickle beasts? Can't we just accept the fact that someone, on a small stage, will break the world in two without even trying?

September 27, 2023
The Grind, Clark University. Worcester Massachusetts

The Albino Mbie Quintet

Before the concert began, the two organizers rambled slightly about how this jazz series began. They said they were hoping for one of us in the audience to give them a ton of money so they can put on more concerts. Surprisingly, no one jumped and wrote out one of those oversized checks you see in Lottery Commercials

But then they announced that they converted the bar in the back of the space to an ice cream bar.in the back and everyone can go and help themselves.

A jazz concert with ice cream? Now I know how to get people to like jazz.

I was being good and stayed in my seat. I was here for music and not for ice cream. Ice cream with a large selection of toppings. There were toppings.

The band came on and was lovely. The singer/guitarist was from Mozambique and brought many different sounds and textures and flavors/

Flavors What ice cream flavor do they have?

Shush. Concentrate on the music.

I am not one to dance to the music, but I was noticing my butt moving around at the rhythms.

I was moving around a lot. I must have been burning a lot of calories. I could spare a little bit for a sweet treat.

As the musicians traded sweet solos, I went to the back bar and went greedy. I put two large scoops of semi melted chocolate ice cream in my cup and then threw in M&M and sprinkles and crushed oreos and anointed it with chocolate syrup..

It was a wonderful gooey mass and I ate it slowly, rapturously.

Oh yeah.

There was music.

That was good too.

It was lively and gave me a sugar high.

I don't know what I was just talking about. The ice cream or the music.

Let us keep some things a secret and applaud with abandon.

October 6, 2023
WICN Studio 50, Worcester Ma
Ricky Kole

The concert was at the studio space at the WICN offices. They are the local NPR station in Worcester and they play jazz most of the time. I listen to them daily. This was part of their Emerging Artists Series. Once a month, a new group of musicians get to perform in this lovely space while the whole thing is aired live on the radio.

I love the idea, but not the fact that it was always at 12 on a Friday. Only those already retired could go. But luck would have it that the school I work at had a half day, so I was able to go.

Yeah.. I was the only person there who was not over 65 years of age. This is not a knock, but a hope that some of these concerts could be done when those who work during the day can go. I know, that's just me being selfish.

At noon, the studio's speaker went on and we heard the NPr newsbreak that they broadcasted on the airwaves and through the internet. The group, one singer and three guys, stood and listened, waiting for the chance to play. They were all young. All of them students at Berklee School of Music.

When the news was over, we heard the DJ in his booth reading the local weather. "62 Degrees in Worcester. 57 degrees in Kansas City. And in North Dakota, the temperature is 59 degrees." What the hell? Did jazz DJs pick random places in America to showcase their weather?

The voice of the DJ introduced the musicians one by one and the singer spoke. She was from Kansas City and she had a relative listening in from North Dakota as well.

Her family was listening to see how she did. They were behind us, leaning in to hear every note.

So the concert was perfect. Her family was acknowledged and certainly excited. We might say that her singing was really accomplished but missing a little spark. We might say that she did not completely mesh with her band that was heavy with a jazz approach that might not be what her soul songs needed.. But we will not say anything of the sort.

We know the temperature in Kansas City and North Dakota. That's all we need to know. Everything is perfect.

October 8, 2023
The Parlour, Providence Rhode Island
Clear Audience

The band played for fifty minutes. They were good. Solid old school bop jazz. It kept me listening. Is there anything we need more from a band making music?

I was caught in a thought of distraction when I noticed a woman standing before. She cleared her throat fro what appeared to be a second time. I looked up and she was holding a little bucket. "Have you been enjoying the music?"

I told her I was. I must tell you. I didn't want to be talking to her about what I liked about the music. I was in the kind of mood where I wanted to listen to music, but not talking about it. "That's great. Maybe you can show that you liked it by giving some money for them?"

I was confused a bit. This place usually has a doorman where the admission to Sunday Jazz is ten dollars. Today there was no one working the door and we all just walked unmolested. I told her that I expected to pay at the door. "Yes. No one was at the door." She moved the bucket slightly closer to me.

I was going to give her ten bucks, because that was what I expected to give. But I was rushing, I wanted to go back to my quite solitude in a half filled bar. I shoved in my pocket and took out a five. I should have rooted for a larger bill, but I just wanted to move it along. With some regret, I threw in the fiver.

She seemed so pleased. Like I just put in a C note or multiple twenties. She was so excited. But I gave less than I was planning. She moved on and I was alone.

But my uncertainty kept me company. DId I just screw the band over? I gave them less money if there was a doorman. But she was happy with the five, like everyone else was throwing in singles, if they were throwing anything all.

Should I have looked for the woman and given her the full ten? But I didn't. i just sat and listened to the music. feeling guilty. A misdemeanor, not a felony. But a crime all the same.

October 14, 2023

Hanover Theater, Worcester Massachusetts

An Evening with Colin Mochery and Brad Sherwood

I did not plan the act of actually going to the concert very well. I knew I didn't want to pay the twenty bucks for the nearby garage and then wait thirty minutes to get out after the show was over. I was going to park on the street. But I didn't plan on where I was going to park.

My son was getting nervous. He just wanted to see the two guys he liked on Who's Line Is It Anyway doing improv. He didn't want to deal with me trying to save money and time by parking creatively.

I wound up on Chandler Street in a not great block. But I parked. It was going to be fine. And then I tried to get the app to pay for the parking space. I couldn't get it to work. I said, "It's okay, I doubt we will get a ticket."

And then we walked by a few gatherings of homeless people on our way to the brighter parts of downtown.

The show was great. It was damned funny. It is astounding to consider that they made all of what they performed up out of thin air. They were clever and we laughed the whole show. That is what you would hope from an improv comedy show.

But for the whole second act, I was thinking about the car. Was it still going to be there? Was it going to be ticketed? Towed? Stolen? I kept on trying to suppress this, but there were times I missed the jokes. Times I forgot to laugh.

My son picked up my stress. As we were leaving he said that the car probably had a ticket. It didn't. It was there. With no ticket. No scratches. Though we did see that I had left one of the windows down.

Not my best performance.

Next time. I am going to park in the garage. The money and the time getting out? Worth it.

October 16, 2023
Vincent's. Worcester, Ma
Genvieve Heyward

I want every band to be successful. Even the bands I don't like. I want all of them to feel artistically satisfied, but also financially taken care of.

I liked this band. I liked them a lot. I would have stayed until the end, but it was a work night and I am lame salary man. But they could have been terrible and I still want them to be rolling in that music business dough.

I don't want to hear that the only reason the band is touring New England is because they have a friend who they can crash with. I don't want to hear about the singer moving home with her family. I don't want to hear that they really need the money from the passing bucket and that they love playing at Vincent's because they get free meatball subs. (They are really good meatball subs)

There is nothing wrong with any of that. I just don't want that to be the reality of being a musician. That there is a very slight chance that they will make it.

But who cares. They are making music that makes me smile. They are doing cool takes on the female centered 70s piano pop. But harder. Faster. And so much fun.

And they shouldn't have to remind me to put money in the empty gas can that was making its way around the room. I gave. I put in ten bucks. I should have put in more because I had some money to pick up a CD or an LP. But they didn't have that. They talked about Spotify. A thing I don't use. I play LPs, CDs and I go see people live. I have no time for the modern age.

I really dug the fact that there were two keyboard players. I dug the fact that Genvieve was in a lousy dress she just picked up at Savers. I dug her tenacity. I dug listening to a band that I felt should be big. The next thing. The last statement.

Every band ought to be super stars.

October 21, 2023

Askew, Providence Rhode Island

Wade Devers and the DBCs

For most of my life, I have taken myself to see my sister play at clubs. She has been a drummer since the time I was eight. I have seen her in punk bands, cover bands, blues bands and bands with singers who were out of tune.

Wade Devers and the DBCs was a eclectic blues band she was in for years. They disbanded when she moved away to Washington. But recently, she has been flying up to Providence to play with another band and figured that the DBCs should return.

This was their first gig in five years and they sounded great. They did a wild version of Moon River.

The whole family was up to see her band the drums. She even worked it out with the bar owner to allow George, my 15 year old son, to be there and hear it all. He really liked it. Of course he did. He was a teenager allowed into a bar to hear his aunt play. This is cool shit.

But for me, I kept on thinking of a time when she was banging her drums in our condo when we were still living in school. She was probably 16 or so and I was younger. She would listen to U2 on her headphones and play along. It got to the point that I could figure out what song she was listening to just from the drumbeats she created.

One afternoon there was a knock on the door. I answered it. It was a cop. I got my mother. The police officer informed my mother that there was a noise complaint against my sister and her drumming.

My mother was aghast. Jen never played the drums in the evening and if anyone asked, she would have stopped playing.

The police officer said that the person who called in the complaint did admit that she never played late and that she actually sounded really good. But their baby was sick and was not able to get the sleep she needed. My mother was getting pissed, "You know, they could have t old us that and my daughter would have stopped right away."

The police man admitted that was true and they advised the complainant that he could have just knocked on our dorm, but he insisted on calling the police.

Jen continued to play the drums only in the afternoon, but now there was a sense of defiance everytime she hit the skins.

And that's what I was thinking of when my son and I listened to my sister play to a well packed bar. She was dangerous behind her kit, but even those who might inform upon have to admit, she sounds damned good.

November 3, 2023
The school I work in. A Charter Middle School, Worcester, Massachusetts.
The Orchestra Teacher.

It is 7:20 in the morning and the kids have already gotten their breakfasts and are talking to each, ignoring the teachers as best they can.

I am walking the halls, checking to make sure everything is going well.

And I hear music. A violin.

I am pretty sure it is a real violin. And it is soaring..

I know the music being played.

It is Bach's Cello Concerto #1 in G Major..I know the piece.

I know it from the episode of West Wing where YoYo Ma made a guest appearance.

It's the one where Josh hears YoYo Ma play this very piece and goes through a PTSD panic attack.

I follow the music. I want to know who is playing so well so early in the morning.

It is in the music room, of course. I enter and see the part-time orchestra teacher playing his violin.

He sees me and stops playing. I am saddened that my presence stopped the music. I should have hidden in the doorway instead of brazenly walking in

He smiles at me and I say, "That's Bach."

"Yeah. It is usually on a cello."

I nod. "I know. I saw YoYou Ma play it on TV."

The guy smiles and goes into a sincere humble brag when he tells me that when he was a kid, YoYou Ma taught him. "I was a child prodigy. Not any more."

He looks at his surroundings, this building that was once a lab facility before becoming a charter school and admits, "But this is the best thing I have ever done. Teaching music here. Better than anything else"

I thank him for brightening my day. And I hope he will go back to the Bach. But he doesn't. He has to prepare his lessons.

And I want to tell him, the hell with that. Get back to the music. Be bold. Make the hallways hum with beauty.

November 3, 2023
The Hanover Theater, Worcester Ma
Get the Led Out

1- I have stated before and I am sure that I will say it again. I don't like cover bands. Or tribute bands. Or bands that only sing one artist's work. It misses the sense of ownership. It lacks the spark of the personal.

2- In 1990, in my first weeks at a new college I saw a Led Zeppelin tribute band. It was the big musical act the University got for the fall. Physical Graffiti.

3- They did the whole imitation schtick. I was in some form of hell.

4- I am not a huge Led Zeppelin fan. I like them. I really love Stairway to Heaven. I know that is a very vanilla answer, but I just dig the song.

5- But my son loves Led Zeppelin. He listens to them constantly on Spotify. He asks me what my favorite songs are. I say Stairway. And he is disappointed. Get used to it kid. Your old man will continue to disappoint.

6- I saw that the Hanover was going to have this tribute band and I hemmed and hawed and got us tickets.

7. Let me say this. I had a good time. They were fun. I didn't once feel like I was listening to moving simulacrums at a rock and roll wax museum. I was listening to a bunch of guys from Philly playing the songs they love.

8.. The lead singer spoke to te packed crowd explaining that they don't try to look like Zeppelin or that they are trying to get it all note for note. They are fans. They love Zeppelin's music. He said the catalog was deep and rich and they were just celebrating the music they love.

9. I got to say, I think that is the solution to the tribute band dilemma. Let them know that you're not recreating. Just that you are

having a good time sharing music you like and that the audience likes as well. This gave me permission to relax and enjoy what they were doing.

10. My son was so happy when they mentioned that there are a lot of great songs they don't get to, but here is one they hope we like and it was The Leavy Breaks, which George adores. He smiled and shouted out, "Yes!"

11. I reveled in my son's enjoyment.

12. When we were walking back to the car, he said to me in all seriousness, "I really liked how they did Stairway. Seeing it live, I finally got it. I finally clicked with the song."

November 5, 2023
The White Room, Worcester Massachusetts
An Evening of Noise Music

5. Before the final act comes, I decide that I should go. I have not had dinner and eight at night feels pretty late at the moment. Also, I don't want the last act to be odd or bad or whatever they can be and blow my good mood. I am leaving on a high, and I better split before it all fritters away like so much feedback and ruin.

4. I only stayed for the two cellists because it would be rude to leave after the talk I had with Sam. I know I will be buying his CD that I see on the table, so I better stick around. The two cellists, Marie Carroll and Rebecca Schrader, are making noise with their instruments. It is a noise show after all. One of them moves the cello's endpin around the floor and they have it mic'd up where you swear you are hearing the ground break in two. They explore all the ways the cello can make noise, or make music or both. Over the twenty minutes I lost my other thoughts and focused on what they are doing. What are they doing? I am not sure, but it has my focus. It has me over a barrel. They end in a moment where they play together and I am there, man. I am there. I applaud. I smile. I get it: The noise thing. It works. Don't ask me how, but it works.

3. It is after the second act and before the two female cello players are about to come up that I hear someone call my name. I look up and see one of the performers from the last group, NxCx. It is Sam Gaskin. I knew him when he was a teenager involved in the poetry scene. I saw him do poetry and I loved how weird his work was. He also makes comics and I have a bunch of his zines and books. I always liked his comics work and have one of his little paintings of a troll up on my wall.. I knew that he did electronic music, but I didn't know that was where he was going. We

spoke about families and jobs. It is hard for me to see him as a man in his thirties when I still remember him as a kid who loved Burger King. I told him I liked his group, which is true. I didn't tell him that it felt like they were creating soundtracks for low budget 70s sci fi flicks.

I mean that as a compliment, but I don't say it because I am not sure he will take it the same way.

2. The first group is done. I am not digging it. It is a lot of repetition and bings and boops. I find myself texting friends. A lot of it is me saying, "Guess what I am at?" Maybe this is just not for me. Maybe noise is just noise. Who knew?

1- I have been sitting here for fifteen minutes and nothing has happened. I am here for noise and no one seems to be doing anything but talking to each other. Everyone but me seems to know each other. Isn't that always what happens to me. I will know nobody here and I will leave not in triumph but in surrender to the disjointed gods of noise music. I ask the guy running the bar area when it is starting and he says, "Well technically, it has already begun. The ambient music that goes with the art exhibit. You hear it? That is the first performer. The pre recorded ambient sound." I do not know if he is bullshitting me or not. I am here for noise and I get malarky. I stop my quiet kvetching, I see the first performer start setting up. The carnage has begun.

November 12, 2023
The White Room, Worcester Ma
Razavaz

The group of four musicians did their first song. They were focused on Persian music and it was lovely. There was a sense of trance music to it. It was almost like an Indian raga. I was charmed and engaged right from the start. The singer sang in Persian, but you didn't need google translate to hear the heartbreak and the longing in the voice.

As they prepared their second song, an older woman in the back of the space stood up and said, "Excuse me. But could you introduce each of the songs and tell us what they are about. Some of us don't know what you are saying. And we would like to know what it is all about."

The lead singer smiled and said, "They are all about love. In Persian, but they are all about love." And they started the next song, which is all about love. Even if it was not about that, it was a good answer to all complaints.

November 19, 2023

The Jazz Festival at Clark University, The Grind. Worcester Ma

The Large Band and Several Smaller Combos

-Here you are.. Trying to write about young artists learning their art.

-You should not be flippant or dismissive at a group of young musicians.

-Being negative to young musicians is a terrible thing to do.

-They are learning. They do not have the chops yet to really shine. They are cocoon musicians.

—You should not expect precision but passion.

-You should see the sparks and the enthusiasm.

-Writing negatively will do nothing but discourage nascent artists, and it will make everyone think you are an asshole.

-Don't talk about the combo that shouldn't have had the drummer that did not keep any beat similar to the rest of the group.

-You should not focus on the absurdity of a school recital for the kids in jazz class being called a festival.

Do not make a big deal over the pedestrian arrangements and obvious song choices by the big band.

-Focus on the fact that the band was able to create something vibrant in their last selection.

-Do not say you wish the whole set was like that, because then you are back in snide asshole territory.

-And snide asshole territory is a fun place to visit, but the sun is hot and it buns your skin.

-Just be happy that the band was gelling. That they found their voice. That they were dancing on the edge of the fierce.

-Remember that new artists need to practice and perform, but they also need people in those seats.

-They need people who will sit through the whole set and clap and smile and give the player permission to try again. To keep on playing.

-You can't always play to a hypothetical audience, the perfect one in your head. No. You need an actual audience that will say, "That last piece you did? That was awesome. I loved it." And let's hope they don't ask you about the songs that preceded that.

-You are the audience. You are their to be entertained, sure. But you are also there to fill up those seats with ears and anticipation.

-You are not the heart and soul of the music. You are the circulatory system. You are the way that sustains the music. To make sure more can be made next time.

-Clap.

-Smile.

-Listen like you mean it

December 10, 2023

The Hotel Vernon's Ship Room. Worcester Massachusetts

At the Second Day of the Punk Rock Flea Market

Captain Vampire

An Open Letter the Gods of Punk Rock (and also to the people standing next to me at the concert)

To those who care.

Yes it is true. I laughed.

I laughed several times during the band's set.

I know that punk rock is serious and that we are supposed to nod our heads in appreciation or slightly bop up and down, but not so much because it's kind of crowded. And we are too cool to show any kind of emotion outside of anger at the Man.

I don't think you are supposed to laugh at punk.

But I did.

I laughed when the lead singer said, "A lot of the songs I write are about history."

I laughed when he went into his falsetto wail at the end of a couple of the songs.

I laughed when the bass player tried to do a little hip sway to the beat of the rhythm but instead lost their balance and had to recover into the cool bass player stance with the hope that no one noticed.

I laughed at the lead singer's negligee/monk's robe costume with the slit up the side so that we can see his shorts.

I laughed because it was a joy to hear the enthusiasm. The pure brio one finds in performing.

I laughed because it was damned fun and damned ridiculous.

I laughed when he seriously introduced his new set of songs about pigeons.

Pigeons.

Why should I not laugh?

Chortle, even?

I laughed because they were over the top and loving it.

They were the joke.

They were the ones telling that same joke.

And it is okay to laugh at the things that require merriment.

We will not leave this place changed or informed.

We will not improve as humans.

But dammit.

We are going to have a good time

December 17. 2023

The Parlour. Providence Rhodes Island

The David Howard Initiative

Dear Foster.

Here I am again by myself listening to Sunday Jazz. Guys our age or older making music. No one is going to find stardom here. But is that why we are here? They need to play music and for some reason I need to hear it. They are good safe players. They are doing their version of George Benson soul influenced jazz. They will not make me swoon or have me remember them in a week. But does music need to stay with us? Can't it have the life of a butterfly? The half life is brief but the colors shine and soar. The music is well done but it does have the feel of background. Like a good arm chair. You might not even notice it, but it is still there in the landscape and it looks damned comfortable. Take a seat. Try it out. Feels good enough. This is safe jazz but on a rainy Sunday do I want danger and unique time signatures? Like the old expression, "Good enough for jazz." Well, it is jazz. And it is good. Enough. Hope you are well. I miss you and other people in the large audience that I know well enough to rush over and embrace.

Yours

Dave.

December 30, 2023

The Huntington Theater, Boston Ma

Yippee Kai Yay!: The Unauthorized Die Hard Show

We had a great time. The one man show was damned funny. He performed the whole movie, sort of. It was just damned fun. This was not a serious piece of theater.

Before the play started, we saw a guy explaining to his date what the story of Die Hard is. We were shocked. Who hasn't seen Die Hard? I thought the guy was mansplaining the story to her. My wife and son thought I was just making a cute moment more ominous. "He was just telling her what the movie was," George said to me.

There was a family near us that seemed to take up several rows. They were not digging it. They sat quietly and never laughed. They spent the length of the play shifting on the seats uncomfortably. And around them, we laughed at the absurdity of it. It was funny. There were things there that made you laugh.

Why would you go to a play about Die Hard and not find the jokes about the movie funny? What a waste of a time out. The tickets weren't too expensive, but going to the theater ain't cheap. Why would you plan to go to a parody show and not be ready to have a good time?

I felt bad for them. I didn't understand them. Maybe I was just too ready to laugh. Maybe I was just an easy mark. We should all be so afflicted .

January 13, 2024
Spillway Company, Brattleboro Vermont
Almost Too Much...Never Enough

A lot of people from the art scene are there. They all hug. I sit by myself in a backrow.. I feel more lonely now than usual. I should be getting used to this.

The show is a melange of improv dance, storytelling and improv theater. It is very naughty and surprisingly good. Everyone is having a good time and it is contagious.

The final part of the show is an open dance. They give the dancers weird costumes to wear and then they have to dance to music they are not prepared for. We get a sexy hotdog dancing to Lady Gaga. It's goofy fun.

But I am feeling a special kind of loneliness available only to unknown audience members and it is at these moments that you tend to be haunted by unexpected ghosts.

While I feel the presence of ghosts, the performance continues. There is one large, overweight dancer. When she goes on to her bit, it is comical. She cannot do a split or a leg raise. She stumbles to the music. It'is funny. People laugh.

And the ghost of Cass Elliot elbows me and says, "This is bullshit. Make fun of the fat girl. I know that they are going to change the song and she will dance triumphantly, but that is small change. That is totally fucked up . Because before we see what she can really do, we get a chance to laugh at her."

For a ghost, she is pretty accurate. The dancer does find her fierce strength when the song changes and people in the audience cheer.

Cass Elliot is not cheering. "Fat girl can sing better than all the skinny girls, but we got to call her Momma Cass. Have her sing that no one is getting fat but her. And they made me sing that. And this girl, why does she have to bring on the jokes before she brings the grace? Can't we be happy with the good dancer? The perfect singer?"

And Cass Elliot is gone. On to other performances to haunt. And I am left with a mostly great night of dance. Mostly. I say nothing to anyone as I leave. Let their own ghosts talk to them about how we laugh, how we cheer.

January 14, 2024
Next Stage, Putney Vermont
Maura Shawn Scanlin

A night of Celtic fiddle. There was also a banjo present. You have to like a band that does not discriminate.

The music was decent. The music was sweet. There were moments of beauty.

It is a good thing that I write these little bits of inter-office mail to the cosmos. If I don't, I am pretty sure all recollection of this night of music was gone. And I don't want to forget it. It was a pleasant enough night of music.

On either side of me, concert goers were knitting or crocheting. There was a lot of fiber arts being made at the Next Stage tonight. I think knitting during a show is alright, but I would rather be at a concert that demands my attention to the point where I wouldn't be able to knit (if I could knit.)

The music was fine. But it was not insistent. It did not hold back the slammed door with a foot wedged at the door jamb. It did not steal other band's equipment and mailing list.

The music was perfectly reputable. This is music you would not mind sitting next to in a crushed rush hour subway car. This music is the workmate you feel confident won't tell stories out of school. This music always has hard candy in their bag.

I want to feel the passion in any moment of music, even if it is a Scottish reel, I want to feel like I am at an early 70s punk concert. I want that beautiful fiddle music to be enlaced with stale tobacco and insistent feedback.

Every type of music has fierce desire as its central core. Every type of music. Except for barbershop quartets. There is no purpose for that nonsense. But for all other types of music. Passion. Go out there and kill everyone of the Irish jigs on the set list. Slay that audience with deathwish precision. And joy.

January 21, 2024
The Parlour, Providence Rhode Island
The Mike Weidenfeller Trio

It is too cold for music tonight. There seems to be little heat in the bar. My fingers are freezing.

Not too many people made it out. That is a shame because the band is quite good, doing mostly bossa nova pieces. Even when they did a Miles Davis piece, it was filtered through a Brazilian filter.

And that is it. I have nothing more to say. Sometimes the music takes you over and you are transported. Sometimes the music assaults you. Sometimes the music stays in the corner and raises his hand and waits to be noticed.

If I did not write this little essay, I would not remember the band.

They weren't bad.

Maybe it was me.

Maybe it was because it was cold.

Maybe because the band didn't clear its throat and sing as vehemently as they should have.

February 4, 2024

Electric Haze, Worcester Ma

An Evening of EDM with Shrimpnose, Daedalus and Vague003

-This evening of music made me feel old.

-Not old like I have seen it all and nothing can surprise me, but old like "Get off my damned lawn ya damned kid."

-I knew Electric Haze did music some Sundays and that seemed to be a good time for me to go out and see something local.

-The featured performer was Shrimpnose who was billed as a rapper and EDM.

-I had to Google what EDM meant. I know. I said I was being the wrong kind of old.

-It's not like electronic dance music is brand spanking new. It has been around in a similar form for over 20 years.

-It is more to do with my ignorance of it.

-When I looked at this lineup, I learned that Shrimpnose and Daedulus are both from California and they are on a national tour.

-National tours awe me. I can't imagine trudging around the country making music, hoping people will show up.

-The fact that they were touring made me want to check it out. See what I was missing.

-When I got there, the opening act, Vague0003, was working the controls. I don't know the right parlance for what they were doing. I left before the final performer, Shrimpnose, was done.

-I never saw a beginning or an end of the night of music. For all I know, this dance music is still going on. Ever hitting the downbeat. Eternal. Rushing from the Big Bang to here in Worcester and then to parts unknown.

-I stood in the sparsely attended evening and saw three performers.

-Old man warning

-I don't know if they were really making music up there. Were they just pressing play on their pre made tracks and adding a little sound here and there?

-I don't really believe that. But I also just could not figure out what they were doing.

-Were they just pressing a few buttons and music is there? I could tell that some of what was being done was manipulating sounds into music right there.

-This is just me, at my age, with my likes and dislikes not understanding how this is music. How this is performance.

-Get off my damn lawn. (If you don't mind)

-All three performers created sounds that had that hard dancing beat, though most in the crowd just stood. A few swayed. One guy tried to dance and gather the crowd with him.

-For the final act, there was a woman with a hula hoop. The hoop had LED lights that created a variety of colors and patterns. I like the fact that they had more to look at then a guy in front of a computer, but I don't know if she had her heart in it.

-I liked the second EDM artist, Daedalus, the best. I could see how he started with random sounds and built layer after layer. He showed us how the magic trick worked and for that I was engaged.

-Shrimpnose, the final performer, tried to get the audience into it by encouraging us to make some noise. It was too late for that.

-I left. The music continued.

-The music is always continuing. Whether you deign to call it music or not.

February 16, 2024
The Natick Center for the Arts, Natick, Ma

Stick Men

What is prog rock?

I am not sure. I know prog rock bands, Genesis, King Crimson, Pink Floyd, Yes, ELP. But that does not define exactly what prog rock is. A video I watched also included Super Tramp and Kansas as prog rock. Okay. I give up. I don't know what it is.

I saw an ad online for Stick Men and tried to get my son to go with me. "I don't like prog rock." He said this but he liked some prog rock. I played him some King Crimson and he dug a few of the songs. And early Genesis, who doesn't love that?

I told him I found out the leader of Stick Men is Tony Levin. I learned he has played bass with King Crimson for thirty years. He has also played with Pink Floyd (after Roger Waters left), Peter Gabriel, Yes and Carly Simon. He played bass on Sledgehammer. He played bass on 50 Ways to Leave Your Lover. He played bass on John Lennon's Double Fantasy album. Even if he didn't like prog rock, he should go just to see some rock and roll royalty.

I did some research on the drummer and discovered that he is one of the drummers for King Crimson and co founded Mr. Mister. I figured I didn't want to explain Mr. Mister and the 80s to him. So George passed on a night of music with his father. Because it was prog rock.

What is prog rock?

No one has an answer.

I went and I had an amazing time. I am not a young man, and I was still younger than the mean average of the audience. It was packed. The trio was amazing. Except for one song, it was all instrumental. It was loud. It bordered on heavy metal, but it wasn't. It was a loud, smart kind of music.

They spoke between songs and all three of them were charming. Tony Levin said he has to check the page while playing. "There is no music written on this paper. It has names I gave for the different parts of the song so I know where I am." God, I love that. .

The drummer was amazing and he played hard. I found myself bopping my head. But no one was dancing. Everyone was in their seats like good little citizens.

Maybe that's what prog rock is. It is good groovy music that you will not dance to.

February 18, 2024

The Prior Center at the College of Holy Cross

Music Program Sponsored by Crocodile River

Bassekou Kouyate and Ngoni Ba

Before the Concert. I found two friends there. I had not seen them in a couple years. I spoke to Michael and we started talking bands and concerts. We are at a concert, it only seems natural that that is what we will discuss.

I told my story of not seeing Miles Davis. "I had a choice to see Christine Lavin or Miles Davis. The Lavin show was the one my friends wanted to go to and it was ten bucks cheaper. The show was great and I was thinking I would be able to see Miles Davis next time. He died two weeks later."

Michael said, "I don't want to do any one upping but back in the 70s, I was living in Rochester and I had tickets to see Cannonball Adderly. He died that afternoon in his hotel room. There was no show."

A gentleman nearby got into the conversation and started doing a lot of "I was at a cool concert" talk. As one does. He mentioned going to a Pink Floyd concert at the Philmore East and Leonard Bernstein being in the audience.

Michael and the other gentleman went on talking about what the music scene in Worcester was like. A lot of great bands were willing to play in small venues.

More tales. More memories. All while waiting for this assembly of Mali musicians to begin. To play music we have not experienced before.

To make us smile. To make us dance. To make us have new memories and new stories to brag on.

February 24, 2024
Hanover Theater, Worcester, Ma
Almost Queen
Deep Cut Amnesia: Some Brief Comments on Tribute Bands
One

A week ago, I went to a concert by the band Stick Men, which is made up of two current members of the long lived prog band, King Crimson. After they performed their first number of the night, which was loud and engaging, the bassist Tony Levin got to the microphone and thanked the packed room for the applause. "For those of you who have never been to one of our shows and don't know us, that was an original song we created. For those of you who have seen us already and know about us, then yes, that was an old King Crimson song, "Larks Tongue in Aspic Part Two."

He received laughter and then they launched into another song that also was new to me. It was all new. I had never seen them before. I would believe anything they told me. If they said that they were doing nothing but later period Bob Dylan tunes, I would have to accept that as gospel.

We don't know what we don't know. We accept the things we are familiar with as old friends. The rest is nothing but tabula rasa. We are walking around in the dark. Maybe that's why we only go to the bands we already love. Maybe that's why we want cover bands more than the new. The shiny. Possibly scary. The things we have not been granted knowledge of.

Two

Twenty years ago, I was at a poetry reading in the lobby of an art movie house when a guy took the microphone and proceeded to passionately perform from memory, a poem about learning that the actress Lana Turner had collapsed. It was great. I was riveted. And he did the last line, "Lana Turner. We love you. Get up!" I loved it.

A few months later I ran into the guy who performed that poem and I told him how much I loved that Lana Turner poem and I wish I could write like that. The guy stepped back from me. He looked at me for a second like either I was a bug or a very stupid bug. He said, trying to hide the contempt from his voice, "I didn't write that poem, Of course that's by Frank O'Hara." All I could say was, "Oh. I didn't know." And I walked away feeling like an idiot.

At the time, I didn't even know who Frank O'Hara was. I have learned. And I have read that very poem in his collected works. And every time I read it or even hear the name Lana Turner, I am filled with shame. There was no reason why I should know that poem. Shouldn't we be happy that there are poems that move us? Must we be initiated on the good art and the good artists before we are allowed to enjoy them? At the time, I just assumed if you read a poem or sing a song and don't say it was by someone else, then it is an original piece. How silly of me.

Three

Yesterday, I took my son to a Queen tribute band. The place, which can take over 2000 people, was packed. We were told by family that this was a very good Queen band. It was a spur of the moment thing and we only got tickets that day. Because of that, we didn't sit next to each other. I had the seat directly behind him.

Sitting next to George was a couple who were so excited to be seeing Queen. Or as close to Queen as possible. The man was chatty to both of us. He and his wife were big fans.

The show started and the band performed Queen. It was fun. They were good. Some of the arrangements were different from what I know of Queen, and I appreciated those differences. But it was all songs we knew. I Want to Ride My Bicycle. Another One Bites the Dust. Flash (He Saved the Universe!).

About fifty minutes into the show, they began to perform a song we didn't know. It was rocking, but it was not anything I had heard of before. The guy sitting next to my son began to move about his seat. He leaned into George and I asked if we knew this song. We didn't. "I thought I knew all of their songs."

"Queen had over a dozen records, there can be some deep cuts from the later albums we don't know.," I said.

The guy nodded and said, "I thought maybe this was their song. The band's song. They were doing a song of theirs just to mix things up."

"Nah," I said. "It's a Queen show. I bet all of the songs are by Queen." The guy seemed placated and went back to enjoying the music, even though he didn't know it.

I became the rude concert goer and took out my phone and googled a line from the song being performed. It came up with "Dragon Attack" which is from Queen's eighth album The Game. It was a deep track, but apparently one the original Queen liked to perform in concert.

I wondered how many people began to wonder if it was not a Queen song. I began to wonder how many people questioned the songs they have never heard before.

Four

We want the familiar. We want the things we know we like.

Even if it is a poem we might like, or a good song by Queen we don't know, we still want the art we have been soaking in.

It's an amnesia for things that are new. Or different. Or sung in an alternate key.

We expect that everyone knows the items we deem good.

The tribute band is a tribute band only if you have heard the songs before. Only if you know the original band. If you don't, then it is all new. It is all wonderful. And frightening.

It is a Schroedinger's Rock Band. In the box is a band who does originals and a band who is dong covers. They exist at the same time. Only when you listen will you know what band it is. Or maybe you won't.

Maybe you should just shut up and dance to the music. Stand in front of your seat and dance. Why not? It's good music.

"Queen Tribute Band. We love you. Get up!"

March 10, 2024

The Press Box, Worcester, Ma

This Guy at the Corner of the Bar with a Guitar

Attention! Attention! Attention!

We have a Code Green Situation!

This is not a drill!

Code Green!

Showing up at a St. Patrick's Day Celebration by Accident!

That is a Code Green!

It is a Sunday and I have a Sunday routine, and 50 people dressed in green at the bar I go to kill time is not part of that routine..

My routine has been established for months now.

I drop my son off at his CAP meeting and then go to the Press Box to write.

There would be 10 people drinking or watching whatever game is on the screens.

And I drink my Diet Coke while they ignore me and I ignore them.

It is a good bar for me to go to while still striving to not drink alcohol. This is a training wheels bar for my sobriety.

But today, I did not hear the claxon call of change.

This is Parade Day in Worcester and that means every bar is legally required to have a Celtic Baccanale..

The place is pretty busy. The whisky is flowing. And there is a guy in the area I usually sit in with a guitar singing the hits. He says that everyone is Irish on this day (something I take exception to) and he will sing all the hits both old and new. But no Eagles songs today. I don't know why but I guess the Eagles songbook is anathema to the Irish spirit.

Too bad, I had the need for a peaceful easy feeling. Ah well. Let's start a fight instead.

He is playing pretty well. He has a decent sandpaper voice.

He started his set with the song Dirty Old Town. He introduced it by saying, "This is a song about Fitchburg." And my addled brain wasn't sure of that. I looked it up and it is a 1949 song about a town in Lancashire, England. The Pogues made it an Irish song in 1985. The song was written for a play because there was an overlong scene change and the song was put there to fill the time.

Every song sung at a bar is there to fill time.

Every song sung at a bar is a way to wait for the next drink.

Every song sung at a bar lets you finally stand next to people who don't feel as awkward as you, or at least they hide it better.

Every song sung at a bar is another shot of white noise to stop you from living with your own thoughts.

Every song sung at a bar is another chance to shout, "Kiss me, I'm Irish," and other lies that seem to make sense. Especially today, when we all are dressed in green.

A beer soaked uniform. A costume for all the singers in the chorus.

Attention! Attention! Attention!

We have a Code Green Situation!

Showing up at a St. Patrick's Day Celebration by Accident!

This is not a drill!

March 10, 2024
The White Room, Worcester Ma
Kirsten Jerme

I don't know when I am supposed to clap. To applaud.

I am here at a solo cello recital and she is very good and deserves clapping. I just don't know if I am supposed to.

In the Bach suite she is performing, she pauses between the movements and there is electric uncertainty of whether you are supposed to applaud or not.

We have been trained to clap.

If there is a pause of more than three seconds, then the song is over and you clap.

Or something like that. This is not written down anywhere. We just learn. When in doubt, applaud madly.,

It isn't just the movements. She finished one piece completely and no one clapped. Do classical music audience members know things that the rest of us don't?

At the end of the final piece of the night, where she played with pre-recorded sounds and music, she stopped. We watched her. Is this the end or is she going to continue? You don't want to be the person to clap when the music is still going on. You will be shunned. You will be banished.

But the musician broke her serious look and nodded and smiled. That was our cue. We applauded like we heard something lovely, which we did.

Near me, a pregnant woman stops her clapping to rub her belly. As if to tell the baby that it is now time to applaud. To clap. No time like the present to learn how and when to show appreciation.

March 22, 2024

Stone Church, Brattleboro Vermont

A Concert Celebrating the Girls Up Front Class Teaching Women Music Production

Match, Orange Peel Mystic, The Dutch Experts

You are by yourself in the same place this year began. You were there by yourself to hear Club d'Elf and now you are here for bands you hope will love.

It seems fitting that this is where it will stop.

The first band doesn't do anything for you. It is grungy pop, or something like that. You were never facile in describing what the music heard is like.

You give weird labels or you say that it was good. Like saying "good" or "not awesome" is a real means to express your opinion on something so basic and necessary as live music.

But this year of seeing shows and writing about it has not improved your skills. You are still just that middle aged dude standing awkwardly in the pack, facing the music.

The band identifies themselves as Match and you are happy to have heard them. You are also happy they are done. Just not your thing. Call it that.

\ As they put their equipment away, the singer's daughter rushes up and hugs her. The little girl liked it. That's all you need to know.

There was then a graduation ceremony of sorts where the eight women who spent three months learning how to run shows were honored. This is good. But you still feel like the outsider. You are at a personal ceremony with no investment in it. The women are proud of their fellow students and the skills they learned. But you are here for music. Even if it is music you will not care for.

The next group is a duo from Boston. The Orange Peel Mysitc is a woman who shouts into a microphone while dancing around her keyboard to pre-recorded tracks. There is a drummer behind her, keeping strong beats.

The singer is about the groove and the image. She has ghost make-up over her eyes. You know it is ghost make-up, because she is selling some of it at the merch table. She is also selling oranges at the merch table. Would she sign the orange if you ask? You will not ask. You don't want to interact with the musicians. We know you.

She has a fan on the floor pointed toward her as she performs. The air from the fan takes her long hair and makes it fly around her like tethered fairies.

You don't care for them either. You like their energy and how kooky the singer is. She is very odd and that is wonderful. If only you also found the music wonderful.

But you should stop thinking like that.

The act of going to music is the important part. Not if you like the music. The going. The attending. The filling of the space with anticipation and desire.

They finish and the audience applauds wildly. You are in the minority with the band. Everyone else had a great time. You should just hide in a corner and let those who want to love it do so.

Maybe you should call it a night. Head back to the hotel.

But you don't. There are two more bands and who knows what they will be like. Will they be the bands you need to hear?

You wait until The Dutch Experts, a woman in a smart blouse and pants set, begins to sing and play the keyboards. You waited for this. It is good actually. But you don't like gothy Cure like music. Never your thing, even when you went to see the Cure years ago, you knew you were out of your depth.

Now comes the moment. The moment of decision. Do you leave or do you wait until the last band? The last band might be the thing. The last band might offer salvation, in any way you would want to define it.

How dedicated are you.

The Dutch Experts began to sing just like Kate Bush.

Okay.

Time to go.

You see that several people in the audience are singing along to her. That's good. That's really good.

Time to go.

It's not like there won't be other bands. Other moments. Other chances to be changed. So many people wanting to share their music with you. So much opportunity.

This book was completed on March 23, 2024.

Appendix

What do you take away from a concert? What are the souvenirs you take from a concert? Does a music concert fit into a hoarder lifestyle?

Well, the first thing is the memory of the music. The things you heard. The emotions you experienced. The way the sound felt as it hit you.

But beside that, there is merch.

You can buy things. It is a sad but true fact that traveling musicians make more money from selling things than performing.

The merch is necessary.

With that said, I am disposed to buying something from the merch table if I liked the music.

I have purchased albums, CDs and one sweatshirt.

Below is a little bit about the things I kept after the concerts.

Club d'Elf. They seem to be the band I have stuck with since I saw them. While I write, I will go to YouTube and find one of the many recorded concerts of theirs. I have a double album of them. I said that I liked the album more than the concert, but now, I think I would want to see them perform live. They grew on me. They are pretty cool.

Isaiah J. Thompson. "The Power of the Spirit" CD. This is the piano player for John Pizarelli. He was amazing. They gave him the spotlight a few times and I was blown away by his skill. When Pizarelli did his merch speech he did something really cool: he mentioned his CDs for sale but encouraged us to pick up Thompson's CD if we were only going to get one. He said that Thompson's CD is great and he just got married. I have listened to the CD a few times in the car and it is a good live recording of piano jazz, which is a lovely thing.

Get the Led Out. George got the sweatshirt. He likes sweatshirts and he likes Led Zeppelin tribute bands. The tribute bands we have seen have merch but no CDs or albums. They can't. But they all have patches and t-shirts and hoodies. It's hard to know how important these things are for them to make a living.

The Screaming Females - I listened to this a few times and it is a good album, though it misses the aural assault of seeing them live. That's always going to be a problem. They blew up the venue and danced inn the ruins. How does a record pick that up. It's good to remind the listener that you will want to see them live.

Genvieve Heyward. I didn't get anything from her. I really had a great time and had money to buy a CD or LP but they didn't have any. They had a t-shirt for sale and a download code to get an album's worth of songs. I just can't do it. I am not the person to listen to songs on my phone. I am an old luddite. I just want to take home a CD. Hell, I would have walked out with a cassette tape and been happy.

Captain Vampire. This is what I was expecting to see more of. A homemade, burned CD of seven songs. The CD was seven dollars. A dollar a song. The recording sounds homemade. It is not an example of perfect production. But it is a folk-punk band. Do we want perfection? Most of the songs were performed in the set I saw, so there was familiarity. I liked the energy of the live performance more, but this is a good CD. At of all of these records and CDs I picked up, this one was the most listened to. I don't know why exactly.

NxCx. This was the CD of noise music that my old friend Sam Gaskin made with his partner. I listened to most of the CD. It is noise music. Maybe I am happier with noise when I am seeing it live. Listening to it the car, I was surrounded by all the discordancy. It's not bad. It is just not for me. And that has to be okay. Why did I buy it? Because Sam is a friend who is out there making the music he cares about, and that is worth ten bucks.

Bassekou Kouyate made a plea to buy the CD from the stage. He said that the band was flying for a show in Los Angeles the next day. And the CD sales would help them. Who am I to not help? The CD is good. I was amazed to hear some of the same numbers he did live and they sounded exactly the same. That doesn't happen often. It makes an honest souvenir of a good concert.

Ork. "Soul of an Octopus" I did not see Ork. They are a Prog Rock supergroup, apparently. The drummer for Ork was the drummer for Stick Men and when I went to see them, I went right to the merch table. I chose not to get any Stick Men albums. That is probably because I was fascinated with this album's cover. It was a Lovecraftian undersea creature all around the other fish. I love this cover. It is so fun. I wasn't sure about the band, but the cover worked for me. The music is prog and kooky. It is a charming album. Phew. That's a relief. I used to blind buy albums when I was a kid. But now that new LPs are 30 bucks, blind buying them is nerve wracking. This one turned out okay.

The David Horwitz Initiative. When I saw them perform, one of the musicians was talking about the project during the intermission. He told his friend that they met for several days and rehearsed what they were going to perform and recorded their rehearsals, and that became the album. I was intrigued by this method, to make an album as a byproduct of prepping for a performance. The music live was restive. It was good, but remote. The album is the same thing. I am glad I have it, but it is not one I will be playing a lot.

I might have purchased one of the albums for sale at the last concert I went to, the Women Up Front Show. Some had CDs. Others had LPs, which I still love and adore and am prone to buy. But they were not accepting cash. It was all Venmo. That is the move. The way things are going. I think I have Venmo, but was racked with uncertainty with it. I also didn't want to ask the person at the table how to do it. Nope. Also, I didn't care much for the bands. And yet, I was still enticed to get something. Maybe it is my idea of tipping the musicians. Giving a tithe to the Church of the Backbeat.

About the Writer

David is a writer of short books. He has over 100 eBooks available for download. Some are cool. He has written memoirs such as: My Life in the Frank-n-Furter Cult, 100 Monsters, Century Bookshelf, I Kind of Knew Edward Gorey, and Reading and Walking. He has written books about pop culture such as Mama Cass's Golden Caramel Bar (about Scooby Doo) and In This Reality (about a Tom Petty music video) as well as a dozen short novels including: Delivery and Third Floor Office. David also wrote the books Gin and Tonics Across Worcester and Letters from the Drinking Town. He hosted several spoken word open mics for over a decade, writing about the process in: Poetry in Bars and Long Play Poetry. He has been a monthly columnist for Worcester Magazine for several years.

About the Book

You are the audience

You are the one who is out listening and clapping.

You are there with the stamp on your hand to prove that you can drink.

You are the one who knows the music.

The most important part of seeing a performance, having an audience.

And that is you.

Without you, there would be no music, no theater, no dance.

You are the linchpin with a cover charge.

Join David Macpherson for a year of going out and seeing shows.

He shares with you what it was like to be at the venues. To navigate the rules of concert going.

The focus is on the audience, not as much on the performer.

Because we know who the important one is.

The necessary one.

The guy in the front row, listening like it means something.

Pick up this book. It will remind you of the joy of going out to see a show.